FAMOUS CHILDHOODS

Johann Sebastian
BACH

Barrie Carson Turner

Chrysalis Education

US publication copyright © 2003 Chrysalis Education.

International copyright reserved in all countries.
No part of this book may be reproduced in any
form without written permission from the publisher.

Distributed in the United States by
Smart Apple Media
1980 Lookout Drive
North Mankato, MN 56003

Copyright © Chrysalis Books PLC 2003
Text by Barrie Carson Turner

ISBN 1-59389-113-X

Library of Congress Control Number: 2003104920

Editorial Manager: Joyce Bentley
Senior Editor: Sarah Nunn
Picture Researcher: Jenny Barlow
Produced by Tall Tree Ltd
Editor: Jon Richards
Designer: Ed Simkins
Consultant: Yvonne Dix

Printed in China

10 9 8 7 6 5 4 3 2 1

PICTURE CREDITS

All reasonable efforts have been made to trace the relevant
copyright holders of the images contained within this book.
If we were unable to reach you, please contact Chrysalis Books.

B = bottom; C = center; L = left; R = right; T = top.
Cover *background* Hulton Archive *front* Elias Gottlob Haussmann
portrait, 1748, courtesy of William H. Scheide, Princeton, New
Jersey *back* AKG London **1** (see cover *back*) **2** AKG London **4** AKG
London **5** *T* AKG London/Deutsche Staatsbibliothek, Berlin *B* AKG
London **6** AKG London **7** *T* and *B* AKG London **8** AKG London **9** *L*
The Art Archive/Galleria degli Uffizi, Florence/Dagli Orti (A) *R* The
Art Archive/Rosenborg Castle, Copenhagen/Dagli Orti (A) **10** (see
cover *back*) **11** *T* The Art Archive/Musée du Louvre, Paris/Dagli Orti
(A) *B* Chrysalis Images **12** The Art Archive/Bibliotheque des Arts
Decoratifs, Paris/Dagli Orti **13** *T* (see 12) *B* Hulton Archive **14** AKG
London **15** *T* AKG London *B* (see 2) **16** Corbis **17** *T* (see cover
background) *B* The Art Archive/Bach House, Leipzig/Dagli Orti (A)
18 AKG London **19** *T* AKG London/Erich Lessing/Musée du Louvre,
Paris *B* AKG London **20** The Art Archive/Bach House, Leipzig/Dagli
Orti (A) **21** *T* The Art Archive/Musée Carnavalet, Paris/Dagli Orti *B*
Mary Evans Picture Library **22** The Art Archive/Society Of The
Friends Of Music, Vienna/Dagli Orti (A) **23** *T* AKG London/Museum
fuer Hamburgische Geshicte, Hamburg *B* Hulton Archive **24** AKG
London **25** *T* Corbis /Wolfgang Kaehler *B* AKG London **26** Hulton
Archive **27** *T* and *B* AKG London **28** (see cover *front*) **29** AKG
London/Werner Unfug **30** (see 23 *T*) **31** (see 20).

CONTENTS

THE BACH FAMILY

The Bach family lived in Eisenach, Germany. In 1668, Johann Sebastian's father, Johann Ambrosius Bach (1645-1695), married Maria Elizabeth Lämmerhirt (1644-1694), the daughter of a respectable merchant from nearby Erfurt. Johann Ambrosius was a member of the largest family of musicians in music history. At the birth of Johann Ambrosius, the Bach name stretched back 100 years. After his death, it continued into the future for another 150.

◄ Johann Hans Bach (c.1555-1615) worked as a traveling violinist.

JOHANN HANS BACH
One of the earliest recorded members of the Bach family was Johann Hans, who was born around 1555. He was related to the great-grandfather of Johann Ambrosius, who was called Veit Bach.

JOHANN AMBROSIUS BACH

Johann Ambrosius was a performer, composer, and director of music for the town of Eisenach. He organized music for the court, the town's churches, and all official occasions.

▶ *Johann Ambrosius Bach played the flute, violin, viola, trumpet, and keyboard.*

EISENACH

The town of Eisenach was governed by a wealthy duke. Music was an important part of the duke's household, and many Eisenach people, including several Bach family members, were employed by him as musicians.

▼ *Eisenach as it appeared in the 17th century.*

A GENIUS IN THE MAKING

Johann Sebastian was lucky to have such a skilled musician as a father. Throughout his childhood, Johann Sebastian was surrounded by every kind of music making.

Johann is Born

Johann Sebastian Bach was born on March 21, 1685 into a bustling, busy household that included the apprentices and assistants of Johann Ambrosius, as well as the family's domestic servants. Johann Sebastian was the eighth and last child to be born into the Bach family, although only five children, four boys and a girl, survived to adulthood.

Bach Museum

About 100 years ago, an old house in Eisenach was refurbished to look like the original Bach family home and turned into a museum.

▶ *This picture shows the Bach Museum in Eisenach. The original Bach house is no longer standing.*

A GENIUS IN THE MAKING

Johann Ambrosius had a cousin who was organist at St. George's Church in Eisenach. It was here that Johann Sebastian first heard the organ.

Musical household

With Johann Ambrosius working as a professional musician, the house was always filled with instruments and the sounds of people playing them.

◀ *Johann Ambrosius earned a good living as a musician, and the Bach family was fairly well-off.*

Family church

On March 23, 1685, Johann Sebastian was baptized at St. George's Church in Eisenach. The other members of the family, including his elder brothers Christoph, Balthasar, and Jacob, had also been baptized here. Johann's christian names were given to him by his two godfathers, Johann Georg Koch and Sebastian Nagel.

▶ *Inside St. George's Church, Eisenach, where Johann Sebastian was baptized.*

SCHOOL BEGINS

There was never any shortage of work for musicians in Eisenach or throughout Germany. The princes, dukes, and counts who ruled the country all had orchestras, and nearly every town had its own band. But Johann Ambrosius also knew the importance of a good education, and he was determined to send his children to school.

SCHOOL DAYS

At the age of seven or eight, Johann was sent to the local primary school in Eisenach, the Lateinschule. It appears that Johann Sebastian was advanced for his age, as he was placed in the same class as his 11-year-old brother Jacob.

► *The school records show that Johann Sebastian was frequently absent from school. Nevertheless, he did well in his studies.*

A GENIUS IN THE MAKING

The busy and musical Bach household was the perfect place for Johann Sebastian to learn about instruments and their sounds. He went on to write music for almost every instrument of his day.

AN EARLY START

Regardless of the weather, Johann Sebastian had to rise early to get to school by seven o'clock in winter. And in the summer, school began even earlier—at six o'clock!

▶ *A German winter scene from the 17th century.*

MARTIN LUTHER

Johann Sebastian's school had a distinguished alumnus who had been a pupil there 200 years earlier—Martin Luther. In 1521, Luther hid from his enemies in Wartburg Castle near Eisenach, where he translated the new testament into German.

◀ *Martin Luther (1483-1546) was responsible for the establishment of the Protestant Church.*

MUSIC LESSONS

In Eisenach and the surrounding area, it was understood that if you were a Bach and male, you would be a musician. Furthermore, as a Bach, you would be respected as a musician. So it was not surprising that Johann Ambrosius wanted his sons to follow in his footsteps. As it was the custom for one family member to teach another, it is likely that Johann Sebastian received his first music lessons from his father. It is also likely that Johann was already singing in the choir of the family church, since we know he had a good singing voice.

MUSICAL EVENINGS

As a child, Johann Sebastian was surrounded by music and Johann Ambrosius often held rehearsals at the house. Other Bach family members also hosted musical evenings in their own homes.

▶ *This picture shows the Bach family enjoying a musical evening together.*

STRING PLAYERS

It was important for musicians to be able to play a string instrument, especially the violin. Orchestras needed more violins than any other musical instrument.

◀ *An elegant lady plays a viol while a boy holding a violin waits his turn for instruction from the teacher.*

LEARNING THE VIOLA

Johann Ambrosius taught his son to play the violin and the viola, since all good violinists were expected to be able to play both. If you were a competent string player, you would never be out of work.

◀ *A viola looks like a violin, but it is larger and makes a deeper sound.*

A GENIUS IN THE MAKING

As a choirboy, Johann learned a great deal about how composers write music for voices. He wrote sacred songs and music for church choirs, as well as much grander music for orchestra and voices, such as the Mass in B minor.

TRAGEDY IN THE FAMILY

When Johann Sebastian was nine, his mother, Maria Elizabeth, died. By the end of the year, though, his father had remarried. His father's new wife, Barbara Margaretha, had been married twice before and brought two daughters with her into the family.

A NEW MOTHER
This German wedding would be similar to the scene Johann Sebastian witnessed at the wedding festivities of his father and new stepmother in 1694.

▶ *A German wedding from the 17th century.*

A GENIUS IN THE MAKING

Much of Johann Sebastian's music was written for real-life occasions. He wrote music for celebrations as well as funeral music. In 1718, he wrote a cantata for the birthday of his employer, Prince Leopold of Anhalt-Cöthen.

▲ *Johann Ambrosius was buried at St. George's Church in Eisenach in February 1695.*

DOUBLE BLOW

No sooner had the family recovered from the loss of their mother, than tragedy struck again. Within a few months of his remarriage, Johann Ambrosius died. The family was left penniless, and it was forced to separate. Two children left home, and Barbara took two girls to live with her.

But what would happen to Jacob, aged 13, and Johann Sebastian, aged ten?

MUSIC AT ST. GEORGE'S

The congregation in church at the funeral of Johann Ambrosius may have heard music by Germany's greatest church composer of the day, Heinrich Schütz. But no one would have guessed that Johann Sebastian would be honored with this same title by later generations of musicians.

▶ *Heinrich Schütz (1585-1672) was Germany's greatest composer before Johann Sebastian Bach.*

MOVING TO A NEW HOME

One of Johann Sebastian's brothers, Johann Christoph, was 24 years old and had already left home. He was married and lived in the small town of Ohrdruf, about 30 miles from Eisenach, where he was a church organist. It was decided that Jacob and Johann Sebastian should live with him.

▲ *The town of Ohrdruf, where Johann Sebastian lived with his brother Johann Christoph.*

THE LYCEUM

Once settled in Ohrdruf, the boys attended the Lyceum, a school famous throughout central Germany for its imaginative curriculum. Their music lessons, however, were given at home, as was the Bach tradition. Johann Sebastian received his first harpsichord and organ lessons. With all the changes over the last year, it was an exciting time.

A GENIUS IN THE MAKING

In addition to being a composer and performer, Johann Sebastian was also a skilled teacher. He wrote music for his students to play and learn from, such as his keyboard inventions.

THE ORGAN REPAIRER

There were two organs at St. Michael's Church in Ohrdruf, where Johann Christoph was the organist, but one was always breaking down. Johann Sebastian probably watched and helped his brother make the necessary repairs, and in doing so, gained useful knowledge about the workings of the instrument.

◀ *Knowing how an organ worked was useful to Johann Sebastian, who would be a church organist himself in less than ten years.*

PLAYING THE HARPSICHORD

Johann Christoph wanted his brother to learn the harpsichord for a good reason. He was thinking ahead to Johann Sebastian's professional musical life. To be an all-around musician, you needed to be able to play the harpsichord.

▶ *A harpsichord was used in most pieces of music. In opera, for example, it accompanied the singers.*

PRECIOUS MANUSCRIPT

At the age of 11, Johann Sebastian certainly enjoyed playing music, but it was composition lessons that he craved most. Since Johann Christoph was not a composer and was unable to help his brother, Johann Sebastian began to teach himself.

NIGHT STUDIES

Johann Sebastian decided that the best way to learn about composition was to study the music of other composers. Working at night, he secretly copied a precious keyboard manuscript belonging to his brother. As he copied the music, he examined it closely to see how it was written. But he was caught and punished! In the days before cheap printed music, the manuscript was too precious to be handled by a child.

▶ *In Johann Sebastian's day, all writing was done using a quill, a pen made from a feather.*

A GENIUS IN THE MAKING

Throughout his life, Johann Sebastian was interested in the theory of music and how sounds and rhythms fit together. He wrote collections of pieces, such as the Art of Fugue, *to demonstrate aspects of music theory.*

PRELUDE IN C

The process of printing music was invented over a hundred years before Johann Sebastian was born. However, the quality was not very good and printed music was far too expensive for anyone but the wealthy to afford. Most music was only available in manuscript form—that is sheets of music copied out by hand. This sheet of music, Prelude in C, is in Johann Sebastian's own handwriting.

◀ *Prelude in C is the first piece from Johann Sebastian's collection of 48 preludes and fugues.*

EARLY INFLUENCES

Among the music contained in Johann Christoph's precious manuscript were pieces by the composer Johann Kaspar Kerll (1627-1693). Kerll was the teacher of Johann Christoph's own teacher, Johann Pachelbel, who was also a composer in the manuscript. Perhaps this connection made the manuscript very special to Johann Christoph.

▶ *Johann Kaspar Kerll wrote many keyboard pieces and was a skilled keyboard player.*

LEAVING HOME

Johann Sebastian was doing well in school. At the age of 12 he was the top student in his class, and at 14 he was in the class usually reserved for the oldest children. But the family in Ohrdruf was expanding. Although Johann Sebastian's brother Jacob had moved back to Eisenach, there were now two more children in Johann Christoph's family, with a third child on the way.

CHOIRBOY

It was time for Johann Sebastian to make his own way in the world. Fortunately, luck was with him and he found a job as a choirboy in the town of Lüneburg. However, the town was nearly 160 miles from Ohrdruf and this meant a long journey for Johann Sebastian.

▶ *A choirmaster directs a choir in a 17th-century German church.*

A LONG WALK

Johann Sebastian had no money for the luxury of traveling to Lüneburg by coach. Instead, he had to make the journey on foot.

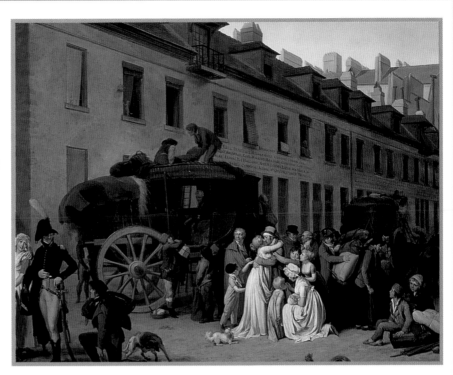

▶ *Coach travel in the 17th century was only for the wealthy.*

A MUSICAL TOWN

Lüneburg was an important trading town in northern Germany, but more importantly for Johann Sebastian, it was a very musical town. It had three churches that were famous for their choirs and organ music.

▲ *When he arrived in Lüneburg, Johann Sebastian attended St. Michael's School.*

A GENIUS IN THE MAKING

Johann Sebastian's musical upbringing in the church gave him his lifelong love of church music. He wrote almost 300 church cantatas, including his famous Sleepers Wake cantata of 1731.

THE END OF SINGING

By April 1700, Johann Sebastian was settled in Lüneburg. Here he received free schooling, a small salary, and a share of whatever the choir made at special services and concerts. It all sounded too good to be true, and for a year everything moved along happily. But then, disaster struck, although it was not an unexpected one, his voice broke!

STREET CONCERTS

Johann Sebastian's choir was called the Matins Chorus, because it sang mostly at the morning services at St. Michael's Church. The orchestras and choirs of the school also sang at street concerts and at weddings and funerals.

▶ *Singers and musicians performing in the street during the early 18th century.*

A GENIUS IN THE MAKING

Violin and string music was important to Johann Sebastian. He wrote concertos and sonatas for the violin and two concertos just for strings—his Brandenburg Concertos numbers three and six.

ROOM AND BOARD

Now that Johann Sebastian's voice had broken, his position of choirboy was at an end. Not only had he lost the wage from being a chorister, but also the free room and board that came with the position. However, fortune smiled on him again. The school was short of string players and accompanists. Johann Sebastian could earn his keep by playing instead of singing.

▶ *As a chorister, Johann Sebastian would have sat with the rest of the school to eat in the grand dining hall.*

SCHOOLS AND CHURCHES

When Johann Sebastian was a boy, schools in Germany were associated with churches to provide a supply of voices for the church choirs, just as they occasionally are today. This picture shows the school and church in Leipzig where Johann Sebastian spent the last years of his life as director of music.

◀ *Johann Sebastian was director of music for the church and school of St. Thomas in Leipzig from 1723.*

A Skilled Organist

Johann Sebastian was now an impressive performer on several instruments, but his favorite instrument was the organ. He had continued his organ studies while in Lüneburg and had made great strides. By the age of 16, he was a competent organist, and he started composing his first organ pieces.

The organ in church

In Johann Sebastian's day, the organ was the most important instrument in church music. In some pieces, such as cantatas, it accompanied the orchestra and led the congregational singing. It also provided background music during the spoken parts of the church service, and this practice still survives today.

▶ *An organist accompanying an orchestra during a church cantata.*

A GENIUS IN THE MAKING

Hearing great organists play gave Johann Sebastian ideas for his own organ compositions. Toccata and Fugue in D minor, probably his most well-known organ piece, was written when he was a young man.

A GREAT INFLUENCE

Johann Sebastian was always eager to study and play the music of great organ composers. One such composer was Dietrich Buxtehude (1637-1707). This Danish composer was the organist at St. Mary's Church in the German town of Lübeck. Here Buxtehude gained a reputation as a virtuoso through his spectacular organ playing.

◀ *Buxtehude was one of the most important organ composers before Johann Sebastian Bach.*

MUSIC AT ST. MARY'S

Buxtehude was the organist at St. Mary's from 1668 until his death in 1707, by which time his playing and music were respected all over Germany. He was important for developing the chorale prelude—a style of organ piece built around a well-known hymn tune.

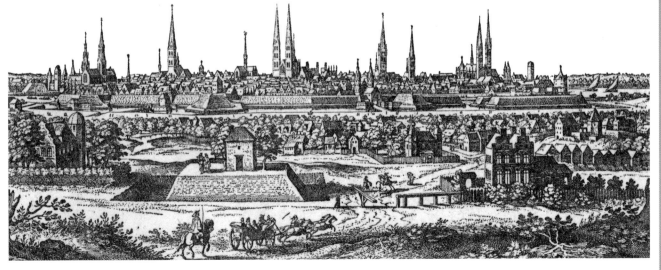

▲ *The town of Lübeck as it was when Buxtehude was organist there.*

SEEKING INSPIRATION

During the summer of 1701, Johann Sebastian had very little performing work to do, so he decided to travel and hear other organists play. Luckily, he had understanding superiors at St. Michael's, who granted him leave. They knew how important it was for a young organ composer to hear the music and playing of other organists.

▲ *Hamburg lies about 30 miles north of Lüneburg.*

HAMBURG

Johann made several trips to Hamburg to hear the distinguished organist and composer Johann Adam Reincken. The elderly composer was already 80, but still at the height of his career and much sought-after as a teacher.

JOHANN ADAM REINCKEN

Reincken had been the organist at St. Katherine's Church in Hamburg for almost 40 years when Johann Sebastian first heard him play. The church services that Reincken played in were filled with music—cantatas, solo organ music, and wonderful congregational singing.

◄ *Johann Sebastian never forgot the exciting organ playing he heard at St. Katherine's Church, Hamburg.*

CELLE

Johann Sebastian also visited the town of Celle, where the court was inspired by all things French and the orchestra played only French music. It was Johann Sebastian's first meeting with the music of another culture.

▲ *In Celle, the local duke had created a smaller version of Versailles, the palace of the French king.*

A GENIUS IN THE MAKING

Johann Sebastian was always interested in the music of other cultures. He wrote French and English suites for keyboard and an "Italian" concerto.

PROFESSIONAL MUSICIAN

In 1702, Johann Sebastian was 17 and his schooldays were over. It was time to find a permanent job. He was delighted when he was offered an organist's position in Sangerhausen, but was miserable when it fell through at the last minute. He was forced to accept another job as a string player.

ROYAL INTERVENTION

The loss of the Sangerhausen job was the result of intervention by the local ruler, the Duke of Weissenfels, Johann Georg II. The duke said Johann Sebastian was too young to be the organist, even though he had obtained the job through open competition.

▶ *A portrait of Johann Georg II, painted around 1670.*

A GENIUS IN THE MAKING

Johann Sebastian's knowledge of church organs taught him how to get the best sound from an instrument. He used different and unusual combinations of "stops" to make the music sound especially exciting.

▼ *The town of Weimar where Johann Sebastian was a violinist.*

COURT VIOLINIST

Depressed by the loss of the Sangerhausen job and with no other organist jobs available, Johann Sebastian was forced to take whatever he could find. An appointment for a court violinist became available in Weimar, and he took it. The music he played was interesting and in the fashionable Italian style of the day, but playing the violin was not what Johann wanted to do.

▼ *Johann Sebastian tested the organ in the church of St. Boniface in Arnstadt.*

A NEW POSITION

Within a few months of Johann Sebastian accepting the Weimar job, an exciting opportunity came his way. He and several others were invited to test the organ of a new church in Arnstadt. Johann's playing at the public recital was so impressive that he was offered the job of organist and choirmaster. At last, his professional music career had begun.

JOHANN'S LEGACY

Johann Sebastian's duties in Arnstadt were fairly light, and he had plenty of time to compose and play the organ. It was the perfect start to his career, which was spent almost entirely in the service of the church—writing and performing church music and directing choirs and orchestras.

▶ *A portrait of Johann Sebastian painted in 1748.*

FAMOUS CHILDREN

Johann Sebastian was married twice and was the father of 20 children, several of whom became important composers, including Carl Philipp Emanuel Bach and Johann Christian Bach. Throughout his life, Johann Sebastian was a devout Christian, and when he died he left a vast library of religious books.

▶ *This statue of Bach was erected in 1908 outside the church of St. Thomas in Leipzig.*

A REDISCOVERY

Toward the end of his life, Bach's style of music fell out of fashion, while a new period of music history, the Classical era, was just beginning. He died on July 28, 1750, and, for over 50 years, his music lay almost unheard. In the early years of the 19th century, however, his music was rediscovered as musicians quickly realized its worth. It has remained popular ever since. Today, some musicians regard Johann Sebastian Bach as the greatest composer of all time.

▲ *Bach's signature.*

A GENIUS IN THE MAKING

Johann Sebastian wrote almost every type of music with the exception of opera. His huge range of music includes keyboard pieces, concertos, passions, oratorios, chorales, and orchestral suites.

GLOSSARY

CHAMBER MUSIC
Music written for a small group of musicians.

CONCERT
When musicians perform in front of an audience.

CONCERTO
In Bach's day, this was usually written for a group of soloists.

FUGUE
A piece of music, usually written for keyboard, in which a tune is played by each hand alternately. In a fugue for instruments, the tune is passed between the different instruments.

KEYBOARD
Any instrument with notes, called keys, laid out as they are on a piano. Keyboards include harpsichords, pianos, and organs.

MANUSCRIPT
A piece of music that has been written out or copied by hand.

MASS
The service of the Roman Catholic Church set to music.

MUSICIAN
Someone who plays an instrument or sings.

OPERA
A musical play in which actors sing their parts and are usually accompanied by an orchestra.

ORCHESTRA
A large group of musicians.

PASSION
A musical dramatization of Holy Week, including Christ's arrest and crucifixion. It is usually performed in church in the week before Easter.

PRELUDE
A small musical piece that is usually written for the keyboard and often used to introduce another piece, such as a fugue.

STOPS
Switches on an organ that affect the sound.

STRING QUARTET
Music written for two violins, a viola, and a cello to play together.

TOCCATA
A fast keyboard piece, usually with a free structure, where the performer can show off his or her skill.

INDEX